Happy Birthda

ANGELINA

by Suzanne Marshall

LiveWellMedia.com

ISBN: 9798609402233

INSTRUCTIONS

* Use crayons or colored pencils (**not markers**).

* Color inside, outside or through the lines - wherever you want!

* Make up your own rules because this is YOUR book.

This book is dedicated to
the absolutely fabulous

Angelina!

You're cooler than ice cream.
You're sweeter than cake.
You're brighter than candles
lit for your sake.

You're greater than gifts
adorned with balloons.
You're loved all the way
to the sun and the moon.

Angelina

ANGELINA

ANGELINA

What gift would a fish and elephant give you together?

Swimming trunks!

Angelina

Angelina

Angelina

ANGELINA

Suzanne Marshall and her awesome assistant, Abby Underdog.

ABOUT THE AUTHOR

Suzanne Marshall writes to inspire, engage and empower children. Her personalized books feature affirmations for kids, inspirational quotes and unconditional love. An honors graduate of Smith College, Suzanne has enjoyed previous adventures as a prize-winning videographer and produced playwright. Discover more inspirational and personalized books by Suzanne Marshall at LiveWellMedia.com.

ABOUT THE ARTWORK

Illustrations included in this book have been curated and redesigned from art at fotosearch.com and freepik.com. Original artists include: © AlexBannykh (cow, goat, sheep); © Clairev (whale) © Dazdraperma (deer, duck, mouse, pony); © Tigatelu (bear, cat, chipmunk, dog, elephant, fish, giraffe, hippo, lion, owl, panda, parrot, penguin, rhino, seal, snake, tiger, turtle, zebra).